The Thinking Tree

PRAYING FOR THE WORLD

A FUN-SCHOOLING GUIDE TO SOCIAL STUDIES, GEOGRAPHY & CHRISTIAN MISSIONS

Melissa Dougherty & Sarah Janisse Brown
The Thinking Tree, LLC - www.funschoolingbooks.com
Copyright 2021 - Do not copy
Dyslexie font

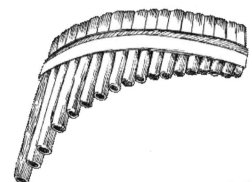

NAME:

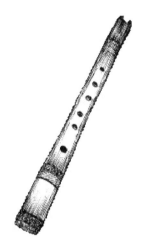

DATE:

Age:

Contact Information:

Table of Contents

Afghanistan	Page 4
Argentina	Page 10
Bangladesh	Page 16
Belarus	Page 22
Brazil	Page 28
Missionary Interview #1	Page 34
Cambodia	Page 36
Chad	Page 42
China	Page 48
Dominican Republic	Page 54
Egypt	Page 60
Missionary Interview #2	Page 66
France	Page 68
Greece	Page 74
Guatemala	Page 80
Haiti	Page 86
Hungary	Page 92
Missionary Interview #3	Page 98
Iceland	Page 100
India	Page 106
Indonesia	Page 112
Israel	Page 118
Japan	Page 124
Missionary Interview #4	Page 130
Kazakhstan	Page 132
Kenya	Page 138
Mexico	Page 144
North Korea	Page 150
Pakistan	Page 156
Missionary Interview #5	Page 162
Peru	Page 164
Philippines	Page 170
Ukraine	Page 176
Yemen	Page 182
Zambia	Page 188
Missionary Interview #6	Page 194
Choose your own country	Page 196
Choose your own country	Page 202
Choose your own country	Page 208
Choose your own country	Page 214
Choose your own country	Page 220
Missionary Interview # 7	Page 226
Missionary Biographies	Page 228

How to Use This Book:

This book will help you learn about 35 countries in the world, specifically so that you'll be able to pray for the people there more effectively. You will use parent-approved books and Internet sites to find information about the country and the physical/spiritual needs of each. You will also become familiar with the location of each country on the map and have the opportunity to get to know some real life missionaries who are currently serving around the world. You will also read about the lives of missionaries whose lives have left an impact on the world.

Learning Materials needed to complete this course:
- Pencils and colored pencils
- Books or internet to learn about each country
- An atlas/globe to locate each country on the world map

Recommended Resources:
- Operation World by Patrick Johnstone
    and website, operationworld.org
- Window on the World: An Operation World Prayer
    Resource by Molly Wall
- Google Earth: earth.google.com
- Joshua Project: www.JoshuaProject.net
- Geography Now: www.GeographyNow.com
- Torchlighters video series: www.torchlighters.org
- YWAM's Christian Hereos Then and Now book series

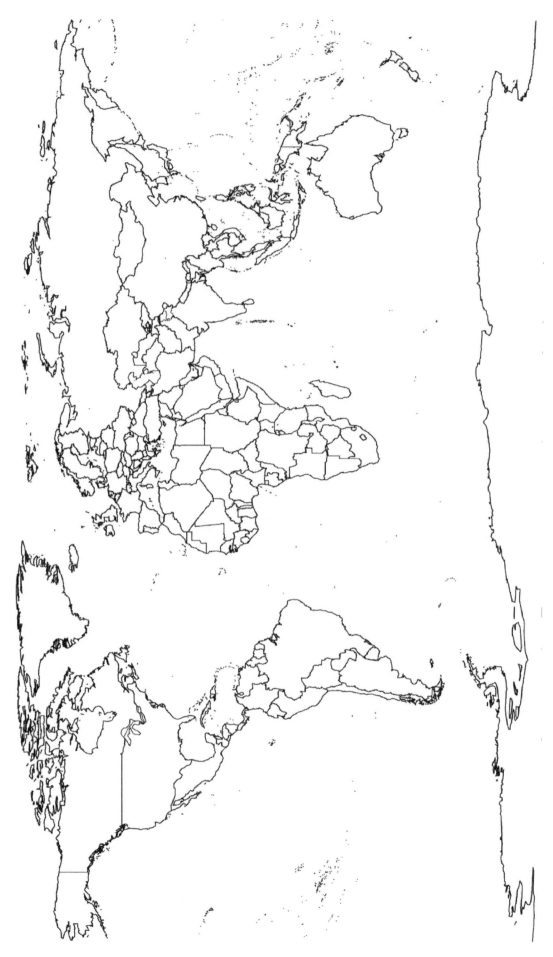

AFGHANISTAN

Color the Flag

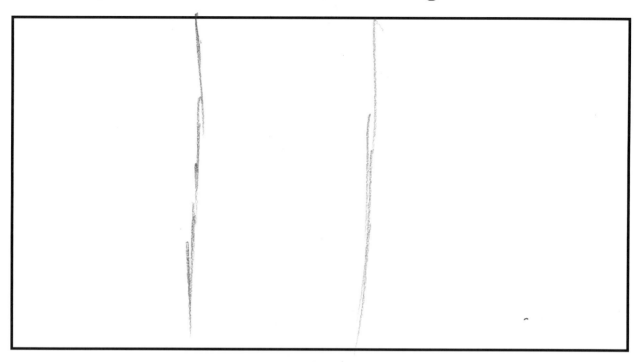

Language(s): Pashto, Dari
Continent: Asia
Population: 38.93 million

Watch a video or read a book to learn more about this country, and write down one unique thing you learned:

Women dont have as many rights as men
The Tuliban have takeing over

What are the major religions present in this country?
What percentage of the population does each represent?

Muslim _____ 99.7 %
_____ _____ %
_____ _____ %
_____ _____ %

What are the main challenges of living in this country?
What prayer needs do the people have?

The taliban people need to be saved by Jesus

What about this country can you praise God for?

I praise god for the missanarys that are there.

Use Google Earth to explore this country! Find the capital city and take a "walk" around. Draw a picture of something interesting you find below.

Capital: _____

Culture & Climate

What did you learn about the culture of this country? Draw a picture below of a unique food, clothing or music that represents this country.

What is the climate like in this country? What are the most notable features of physical geography, such as mountain ranges, bodies of water, etc?

Now that you've learned more about this country, write a prayer below for the people who live there:

_____
_____
_____
_____
_____
_____
_____
_____
_____
_____
_____
_____
_____
_____

ARGENTINA

Color the Flag

Language(s): _____
Continent: _____
Population: _____

Watch a video or read a book to learn more about this country, and write down one unique thing you learned:

_____
_____
_____
_____
_____
_____
_____
_____
_____

What are the major religions present in this country?
What percentage of the population does each represent?

_____   _____%
_____   _____%
_____   _____%
_____   _____%

What are the main challenges of living in this country?
What prayer needs do the people have?

_____
_____
_____
_____
_____
_____
_____
_____
_____

What about this country can you praise God for?

_____
_____
_____
_____
_____
_____
_____
_____

Use Google Earth to explore this country! Find the capital city and take a "walk" around. Draw a picture of something interesting you find below.

Capital: _____

13

Culture & Climate

What did you learn about the culture of this country? Draw a picture below of a unique food, clothing or music that represents this country.

What is the climate like in this country? What are the most notable features of physical geography, such as mountain ranges, bodies of water, etc?

Now that you've learned more about this country, write a prayer below for the people who live there:

BANGLADESH

Color the Flag

Language(s): _____
Continent: _____
Population: _____

Watch a video or read a book to learn more about this country, and write down one unique thing you learned:

_____
_____
_____
_____
_____
_____
_____
_____
_____

What are the major religions present in this country?
What percentage of the population does each represent?

Religion	Percentage
_____	_____%
_____	_____%
_____	_____%
_____	_____%

What are the main challenges of living in this country?
What prayer needs do the people have?

_____
_____
_____
_____
_____
_____
_____
_____

What about this country can you praise God for?

_____
_____
_____
_____
_____
_____
_____
_____

Use Google Earth to explore this country! Find the capital city and take a "walk" around. Draw a picture of something interesting you find below.

Capital: _____

Culture & Climate

What did you learn about the culture of this country? Draw a picture below of a unique food, clothing or music that represents this country.

What is the climate like in this country? What are the most notable features of physical geography, such as mountain ranges, bodies of water, etc?

Now that you've learned more about this country, write a prayer below for the people who live there:

BELARUS

Color the Flag

Language(s): _____
Continent: _____
Population: _____

Watch a video or read a book to learn more about this country, and write down one unique thing you learned:

_____
_____
_____
_____
_____
_____
_____
_____
_____

What are the major religions present in this country?
What percentage of the population does each represent?

_____   _____%
_____   _____%
_____   _____%
_____   _____%

What are the main challenges of living in this country?
What prayer needs do the people have?

_____
_____
_____
_____
_____
_____
_____
_____

What about this country can you praise God for?

_____
_____
_____
_____
_____
_____
_____
_____

Use Google Earth to explore this country! Find the capital city and take a "walk" around. Draw a picture of something interesting you find below.

Capital: _____

Culture & Climate

What did you learn about the culture of this country? Draw a picture below of a unique food, clothing or music that represents this country.

What is the climate like in this country? What are the most notable features of physical geography, such as mountain ranges, bodies of water, etc?

Now that you've learned more about this country, write a prayer below for the people who live there:

BRAZIL

Color the Flag

Language(s): _____
Continent: _____
Population: _____

Watch a video or read a book to learn more about this country, and write down one unique thing you learned:

What are the major religions present in this country?
What percentage of the population does each represent?

Religion	%
_____	_____%
_____	_____%
_____	_____%
_____	_____%

What are the main challenges of living in this country?
What prayer needs do the people have?

_____

_____

_____

_____

_____

_____

_____

_____

What about this country can you praise God for?

_____

_____

_____

_____

_____

_____

_____

Use Google Earth to explore this country! Find the capital city and take a "walk" around. Draw a picture of something interesting you find below.

Capital: _____

Culture & Climate

What did you learn about the culture of this country? Draw a picture below of a unique food, clothing or music that represents this country.

What is the climate like in this country? What are the most notable features of physical geography, such as mountain ranges, bodies of water, etc?

Now that you've learned more about this country, write a prayer below for the people who live there:

MEET A MISSIONARY

Contact a missionary who is currently serving in one of the countries you just studied. Write down three questions you will ask and their answers below.

Missionary's Name: _____
Country where they live: _____

Question 1: _____
_____?

Answer: _____
_____
_____
_____

Question 2: _____
_____?

Answer: _____
_____
_____
_____

Question 3: _____
_____?

Answer: _____
_____
_____
_____

Make sure to pray for the missionary and the needs they mentioned when the conversation is over!

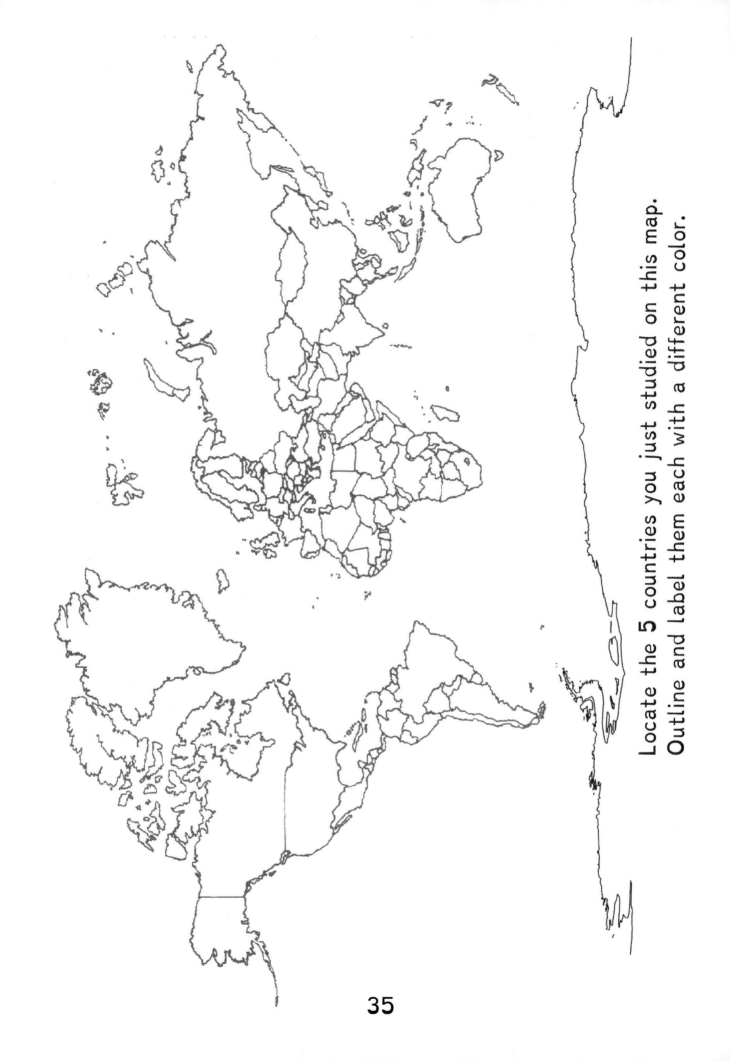

Locate the 5 countries you just studied on this map. Outline and label them each with a different color.

CAMBODIA

Color the Flag

Language(s): _____
Continent: _____
Population: _____

Watch a video or read a book to learn more about this country, and write down one unique thing you learned:

_____
_____
_____
_____
_____
_____
_____
_____
_____
_____

What are the major religions present in this country?
What percentage of the population does each represent?

_____	_____%
_____	_____%
_____	_____%
_____	_____%

What are the main challenges of living in this country?
What prayer needs do the people have?

_____
_____
_____
_____
_____
_____
_____
_____

What about this country can you praise God for?

_____
_____
_____
_____
_____
_____
_____

Use Google Earth to explore this country! Find the capital city and take a "walk" around. Draw a picture of something interesting you find below.

Capital: _____

Culture & Climate

What did you learn about the culture of this country? Draw a picture below of a unique food, clothing or music that represents this country.

What is the climate like in this country? What are the most notable features of physical geography, such as mountain ranges, bodies of water, etc?

Now that you've learned more about this country, write a prayer below for the people who live there:

CHAD

Color the Flag

Language(s): _____
Continent: _____
Population: _____

Watch a video or read a book to learn more about this country, and write down one unique thing you learned:

What are the major religions present in this country?
What percentage of the population does each represent?

_____   _____%
_____   _____%
_____   _____%
_____   _____%

What are the main challenges of living in this country?
What prayer needs do the people have?

_____
_____
_____
_____
_____
_____
_____
_____

What about this country can you praise God for?

_____
_____
_____
_____
_____
_____
_____
_____

Use Google Earth to explore this country! Find the capital city and take a "walk" around. Draw a picture of something interesting you find below.

Capital: _____

Culture & Climate

What did you learn about the culture of this country? Draw a picture below of a unique food, clothing or music that represents this country.

What is the climate like in this country? What are the most notable features of physical geography, such as mountain ranges, bodies of water, etc?

Now that you've learned more about this country, write a prayer below for the people who live there:

_____
_____
_____
_____
_____
_____
_____
_____
_____
_____
_____
_____
_____
_____
_____
_____

CHINA

Color the Flag

Language(s): _____
Continent: _____
Population: _____

Watch a video or read a book to learn more about this country, and write down one unique thing you learned:

_____
_____
_____
_____
_____
_____
_____
_____
_____
_____

What are the major religions present in this country?
What percentage of the population does each represent?

_____   _____%
_____   _____%
_____   _____%
_____   _____%

What are the main challenges of living in this country?
What prayer needs do the people have?

_____
_____
_____
_____
_____
_____
_____
_____

What about this country can you praise God for?

_____
_____
_____
_____
_____
_____
_____
_____

Use Google Earth to explore this country! Find the capital city and take a "walk" around. Draw a picture of something interesting you find below.

Capital: _____

Culture & Climate

What did you learn about the culture of this country? Draw a picture below of a unique food, clothing or music that represents this country.

What is the climate like in this country? What are the most notable features of physical geography, such as mountain ranges, bodies of water, etc?

Now that you've learned more about this country, write a prayer below for the people who live there:

_____
_____
_____
_____
_____
_____
_____
_____
_____
_____
_____
_____
_____
_____

DOMINICAN REPUBLIC

Color the Flag

Language(s): _____
Continent: _____
Population: _____

Watch a video or read a book to learn more about this country, and write down one unique thing you learned:

_____
_____
_____
_____
_____
_____
_____
_____
_____

What are the major religions present in this country?
What percentage of the population does each represent?

_____	_____%
_____	_____%
_____	_____%
_____	_____%

What are the main challenges of living in this country?
What prayer needs do the people have?

_____

_____

_____

_____

_____

_____

_____

_____

What about this country can you praise God for?

_____

_____

_____

_____

_____

_____

_____

Use Google Earth to explore this country! Find the capital city and take a "walk" around. Draw a picture of something interesting you find below.

Capital: _____

Culture & Climate

What did you learn about the culture of this country? Draw a picture below of a unique food, clothing or music that represents this country.

What is the climate like in this country? What are the most notable features of physical geography, such as mountain ranges, bodies of water, etc?

Now that you've learned more about this country, write a prayer below for the people who live there:

EGYPT

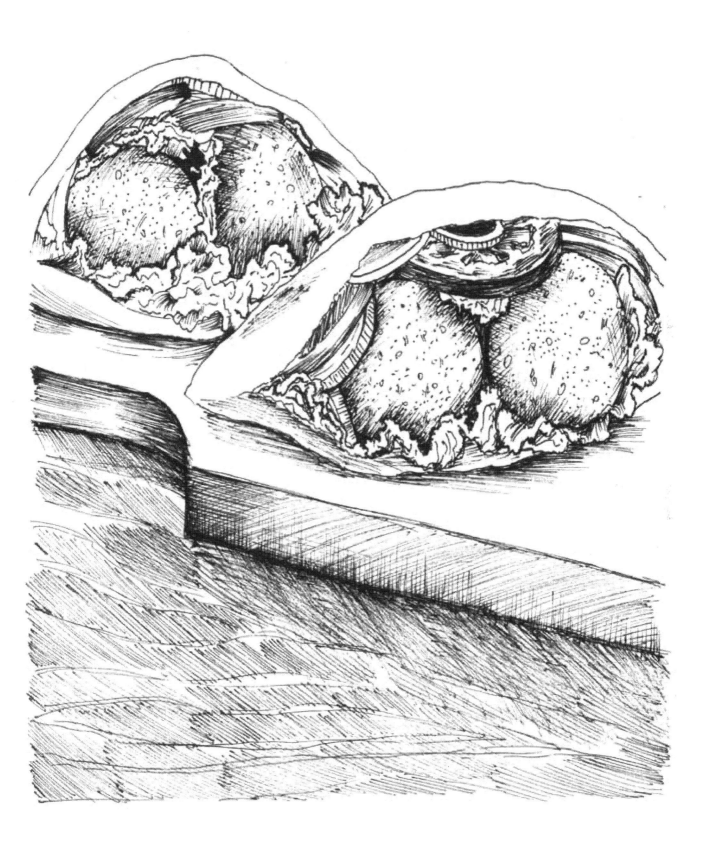

Color the Flag

Language(s): _____
Continent: _____
Population: _____

Watch a video or read a book to learn more about this country, and write down one unique thing you learned:

_____
_____
_____
_____
_____
_____
_____
_____
_____

What are the major religions present in this country?
What percentage of the population does each represent?

_____   _____%
_____   _____%
_____   _____%
_____   _____%

What are the main challenges of living in this country?
What prayer needs do the people have?

_____
_____
_____
_____
_____
_____
_____
_____

What about this country can you praise God for?

_____
_____
_____
_____
_____
_____
_____
_____

Use Google Earth to explore this country! Find the capital city and take a "walk" around. Draw a picture of something interesting you find below.

Capital: _____

Culture & Climate

What did you learn about the culture of this country? Draw a picture below of a unique food, clothing or music that represents this country.

What is the climate like in this country? What are the most notable features of physical geography, such as mountain ranges, bodies of water, etc?

Now that you've learned more about this country, write a prayer below for the people who live there:

_____
_____
_____
_____
_____
_____
_____
_____
_____
_____
_____
_____
_____
_____
_____
_____
_____

MEET A MISSIONARY

Contact a missionary who is currently serving in one of the countries you just studied. Write down three questions you will ask and their answers below.

Missionary's Name: _____
Country where they live: _____

Question 1: _____
_____?

Answer: _____
_____
_____
_____

Question 2: _____
_____?

Answer: _____
_____
_____
_____

Question 3: _____
_____?

Answer: _____
_____
_____
_____

Make sure to pray for the missionary and the needs they mentioned when the conversation is over!

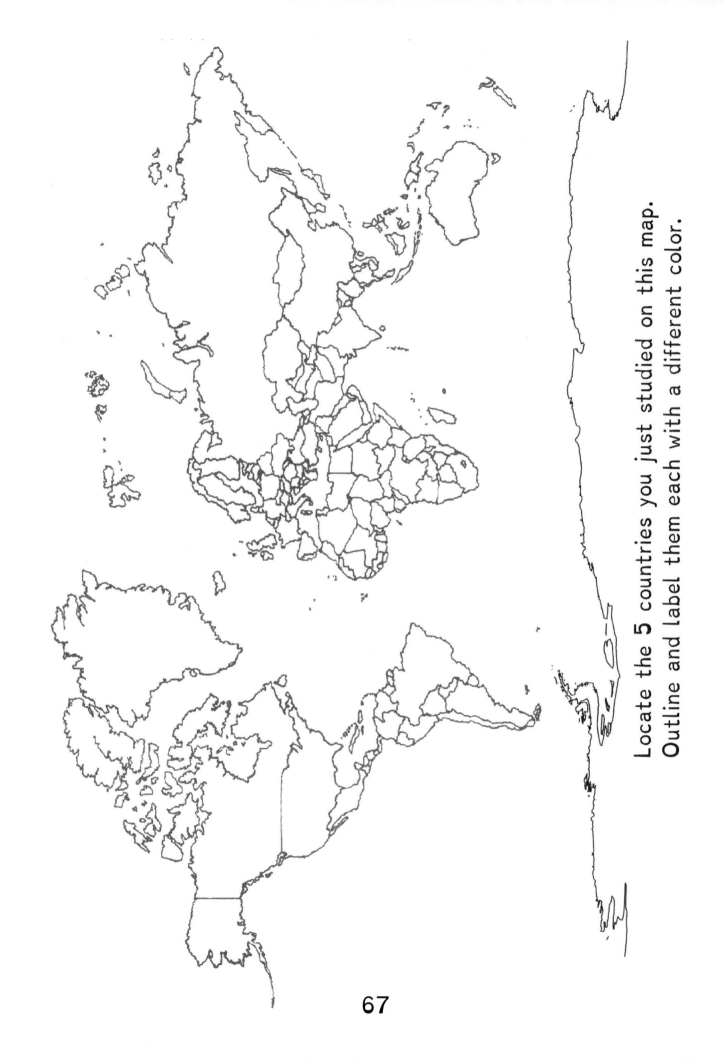

Locate the 5 countries you just studied on this map. Outline and label them each with a different color.

FRANCE

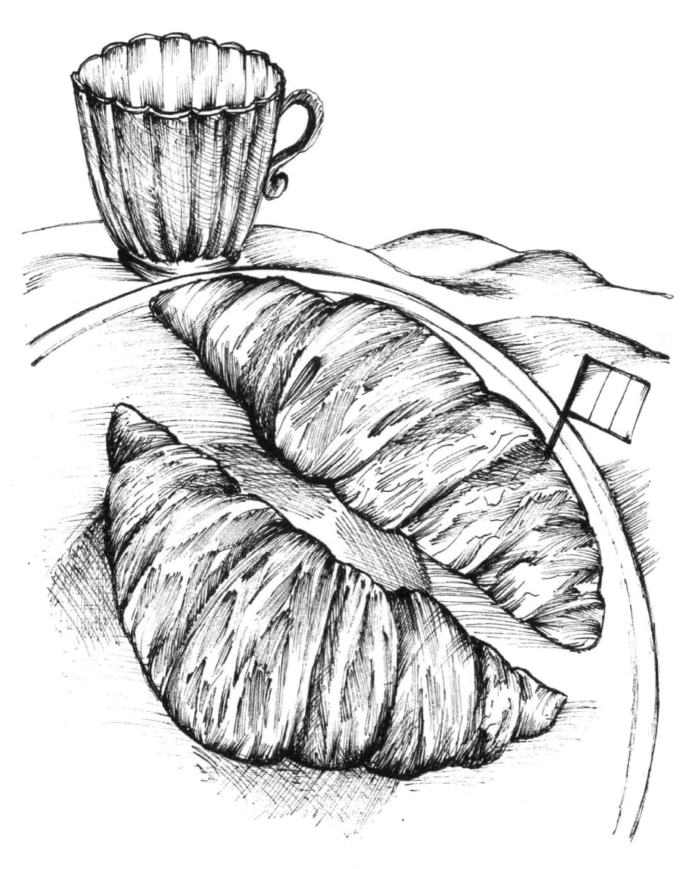

Color the Flag

Language(s): _____
Continent: _____
Population: _____

Watch a video or read a book to learn more about this country, and write down one unique thing you learned:

_____
_____
_____
_____
_____
_____
_____
_____
_____

What are the major religions present in this country?
What percentage of the population does each represent?

_____   _____%
_____   _____%
_____   _____%
_____   _____%

What are the main challenges of living in this country?
What prayer needs do the people have?

_____
_____
_____
_____
_____
_____
_____
_____

What about this country can you praise God for?

_____
_____
_____
_____
_____
_____
_____
_____

Use Google Earth to explore this country! Find the capital city and take a "walk" around. Draw a picture of something interesting you find below.

Capital: _____

Culture & Climate

What did you learn about the culture of this country? Draw a picture below of a unique food, clothing or music that represents this country.

What is the climate like in this country? What are the most notable features of physical geography, such as mountain ranges, bodies of water, etc?

Now that you've learned more about this country, write a prayer below for the people who live there:

_____
_____
_____
_____
_____
_____
_____
_____
_____
_____
_____
_____
_____
_____
_____

GREECE

Color the Flag

Language(s): _____
Continent: _____
Population: _____

Watch a video or read a book to learn more about this country, and write down one unique thing you learned:

_____
_____
_____
_____
_____
_____
_____
_____
_____
_____

What are the major religions present in this country?
What percentage of the population does each represent?

_____   _____%
_____   _____%
_____   _____%
_____   _____%

What are the main challenges of living in this country?
What prayer needs do the people have?

_____
_____
_____
_____
_____
_____
_____
_____

What about this country can you praise God for?

_____
_____
_____
_____
_____
_____
_____

Use Google Earth to explore this country! Find the capital city and take a "walk" around. Draw a picture of something interesting you find below.

Capital: _____

Culture & Climate

What did you learn about the culture of this country? Draw a picture below of a unique food, clothing or music that represents this country.

What is the climate like in this country? What are the most notable features of physical geography, such as mountain ranges, bodies of water, etc?

Now that you've learned more about this country, write a prayer below for the people who live there:

_____
_____
_____
_____
_____
_____
_____
_____
_____
_____
_____
_____
_____
_____
_____
_____

GUATEMALA

Color the Flag

Language(s): _____
Continent: _____
Population: _____

Watch a video or read a book to learn more about this country, and write down one unique thing you learned:

_____
_____
_____
_____
_____
_____
_____
_____
_____

What are the major religions present in this country?
What percentage of the population does each represent?

_____   _____%
_____   _____%
_____   _____%
_____   _____%

What are the main challenges of living in this country?
What prayer needs do the people have?

_____
_____
_____
_____
_____
_____
_____
_____

What about this country can you praise God for?

_____
_____
_____
_____
_____
_____
_____

Use Google Earth to explore this country! Find the capital city and take a "walk" around. Draw a picture of something interesting you find below.

Capital: _____

Culture & Climate

What did you learn about the culture of this country? Draw a picture below of a unique food, clothing or music that represents this country.

What is the climate like in this country? What are the most notable features of physical geography, such as mountain ranges, bodies of water, etc?

Now that you've learned more about this country, write a prayer below for the people who live there:

_____
_____
_____
_____
_____
_____
_____
_____
_____
_____
_____
_____
_____
_____
_____

HAITI

Color the Flag

Language(s): _____
Continent: _____
Population: _____

Watch a video or read a book to learn more about this country, and write down one unique thing you learned:

_____
_____
_____
_____
_____
_____
_____
_____
_____
_____

What are the major religions present in this country?
What percentage of the population does each represent?

_____   _____%
_____   _____%
_____   _____%
_____   _____%

What are the main challenges of living in this country?
What prayer needs do the people have?

_____
_____
_____
_____
_____
_____
_____
_____
_____

What about this country can you praise God for?

_____
_____
_____
_____
_____
_____
_____
_____

Use Google Earth to explore this country! Find the capital city and take a "walk" around. Draw a picture of something interesting you find below.

Capital: _____

Culture & Climate

What did you learn about the culture of this country? Draw a picture below of a unique food, clothing or music that represents this country.

What is the climate like in this country? What are the most notable features of physical geography, such as mountain ranges, bodies of water, etc?

Now that you've learned more about this country, write a prayer below for the people who live there:

_____
_____
_____
_____
_____
_____
_____
_____
_____
_____
_____
_____
_____
_____
_____

HUNGARY

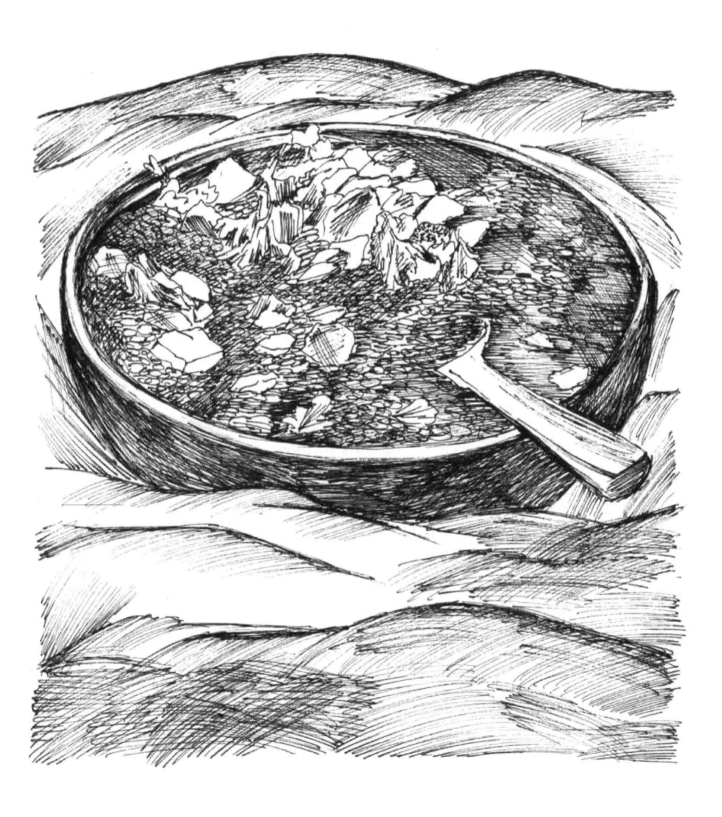

Color the Flag

Language(s): _____
Continent: _____
Population: _____

Watch a video or read a book to learn more about this country, and write down one unique thing you learned:

What are the major religions present in this country?
What percentage of the population does each represent?

_____   _____%
_____   _____%
_____   _____%
_____   _____%

What are the main challenges of living in this country?
What prayer needs do the people have?

_____
_____
_____
_____
_____
_____
_____
_____

What about this country can you praise God for?

_____
_____
_____
_____
_____
_____
_____

Use Google Earth to explore this country! Find the capital city and take a "walk" around. Draw a picture of something interesting you find below.

Capital: _____

Culture & Climate

What did you learn about the culture of this country? Draw a picture below of a unique food, clothing or music that represents this country.

What is the climate like in this country? What are the most notable features of physical geography, such as mountain ranges, bodies of water, etc?

Now that you've learned more about this country, write a prayer below for the people who live there:

_____
_____
_____
_____
_____
_____
_____
_____
_____
_____
_____
_____
_____
_____
_____
_____
_____

MEET A MISSIONARY

Contact a missionary who is currently serving in one of the countries you just studied. Write down three questions you will ask and their answers below.

Missionary's Name: _____
Country where they live: _____

Question 1: _____
_____?

Answer: _____
_____
_____
_____

Question 2: _____
_____?

Answer: _____
_____
_____
_____

Question 3: _____
_____?

Answer: _____
_____
_____
_____

Make sure to pray for the missionary and the needs they mentioned when the conversation is over!

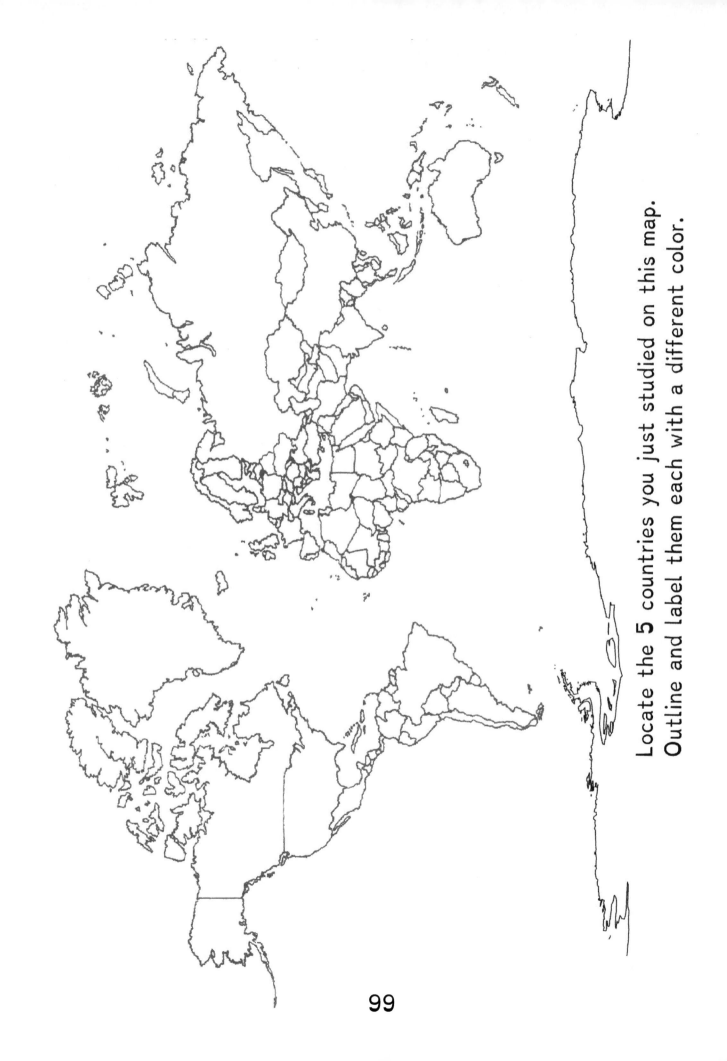

ICELAND

Color the Flag

Language(s): _____
Continent: _____
Population: _____

Watch a video or read a book to learn more about this country, and write down one unique thing you learned:

_____
_____
_____
_____
_____
_____
_____
_____
_____
_____

What are the major religions present in this country?
What percentage of the population does each represent?

_____	_____%
_____	_____%
_____	_____%
_____	_____%

What are the main challenges of living in this country?
What prayer needs do the people have?

_____
_____
_____
_____
_____
_____
_____
_____

What about this country can you praise God for?

_____
_____
_____
_____
_____
_____
_____

Use Google Earth to explore this country! Find the capital city and take a "walk" around. Draw a picture of something interesting you find below.

Capital: _____

Culture & Climate

What did you learn about the culture of this country? Draw a picture below of a unique food, clothing or music that represents this country.

What is the climate like in this country? What are the most notable features of physical geography, such as mountain ranges, bodies of water, etc?

Now that you've learned more about this country, write a prayer below for the people who live there:

_____
_____
_____
_____
_____
_____
_____
_____
_____
_____
_____
_____
_____
_____

INDIA

Color the Flag

Language(s): _____
Continent: _____
Population: _____

Watch a video or read a book to learn more about this country, and write down one unique thing you learned:

_____
_____
_____
_____
_____
_____
_____
_____
_____

What are the major religions present in this country?
What percentage of the population does each represent?

_____   _____%
_____   _____%
_____   _____%
_____   _____%

What are the main challenges of living in this country?
What prayer needs do the people have?

_____
_____
_____
_____
_____
_____
_____
_____

What about this country can you praise God for?

_____
_____
_____
_____
_____
_____
_____

Use Google Earth to explore this country! Find the capital city and take a "walk" around. Draw a picture of something interesting you find below.

Capital: _____

Culture & Climate

What did you learn about the culture of this country? Draw a picture below of a unique food, clothing or music that represents this country.

What is the climate like in this country? What are the most notable features of physical geography, such as mountain ranges, bodies of water, etc?

Now that you've learned more about this country, write a prayer below for the people who live there:

_____
_____
_____
_____
_____
_____
_____
_____
_____
_____
_____
_____
_____
_____
_____
_____
_____
_____

INDONESIA

Color the Flag

Language(s): _____
Continent: _____
Population: _____

Watch a video or read a book to learn more about this country, and write down one unique thing you learned:

_____
_____
_____
_____
_____
_____
_____
_____
_____

What are the major religions present in this country?
What percentage of the population does each represent?

_____   _____%
_____   _____%
_____   _____%
_____   _____%

What are the main challenges of living in this country?
What prayer needs do the people have?

_____
_____
_____
_____
_____
_____
_____
_____
_____

What about this country can you praise God for?

_____
_____
_____
_____
_____
_____
_____
_____

Use Google Earth to explore this country! Find the capital city and take a "walk" around. Draw a picture of something interesting you find below.

Capital: _____

Culture & Climate

What did you learn about the culture of this country? Draw a picture below of a unique food, clothing or music that represents this country.

What is the climate like in this country? What are the most notable features of physical geography, such as mountain ranges, bodies of water, etc?

Now that you've learned more about this country, write a prayer below for the people who live there:

ISRAEL

Color the Flag

Language(s): _____
Continent: _____
Population: _____

Watch a video or read a book to learn more about this country, and write down one unique thing you learned:

_____
_____
_____
_____
_____
_____
_____
_____
_____

What are the major religions present in this country?
What percentage of the population does each represent?

_____   _____%
_____   _____%
_____   _____%
_____   _____%

What are the main challenges of living in this country?
What prayer needs do the people have?

_____
_____
_____
_____
_____
_____
_____
_____
_____

What about this country can you praise God for?

_____
_____
_____
_____
_____
_____
_____
_____
_____

Use Google Earth to explore this country! Find the capital city and take a "walk" around. Draw a picture of something interesting you find below.

Capital: _____

Culture & Climate

What did you learn about the culture of this country? Draw a picture below of a unique food, clothing or music that represents this country.

What is the climate like in this country? What are the most notable features of physical geography, such as mountain ranges, bodies of water, etc?

Now that you've learned more about this country, write a prayer below for the people who live there:

JAPAN

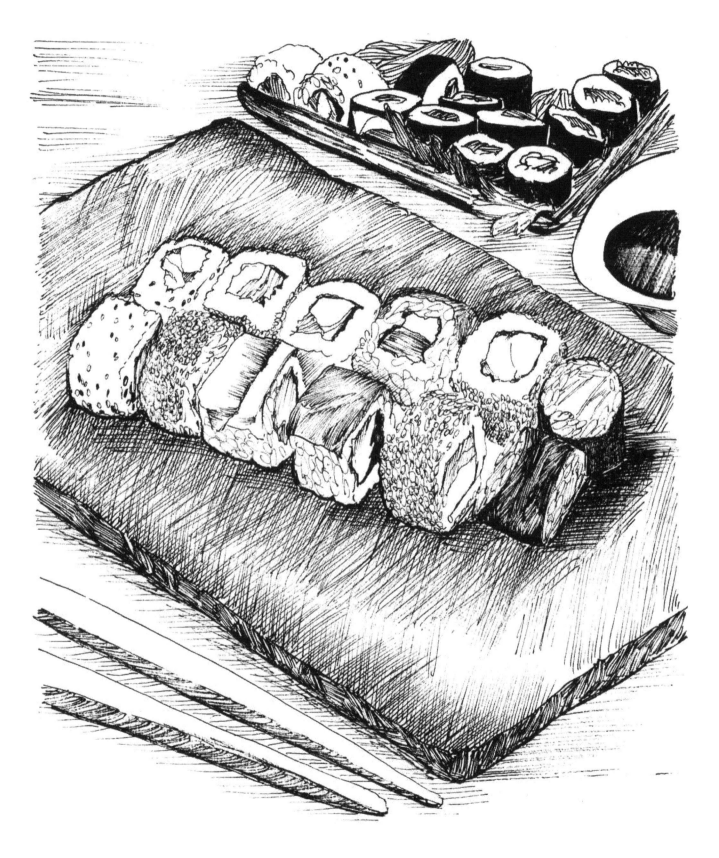

Color the Flag

Language(s): _____
Continent: _____
Population: _____

Watch a video or read a book to learn more about this country, and write down one unique thing you learned:

_____
_____
_____
_____
_____
_____
_____
_____
_____

What are the major religions present in this country?
What percentage of the population does each represent?

_____   _____%
_____   _____%
_____   _____%
_____   _____%

What are the main challenges of living in this country?
What prayer needs do the people have?

_____
_____
_____
_____
_____
_____
_____
_____
_____

What about this country can you praise God for?

_____
_____
_____
_____
_____
_____
_____
_____

Use Google Earth to explore this country! Find the capital city and take a "walk" around. Draw a picture of something interesting you find below.

Capital: _____

Culture & Climate

What did you learn about the culture of this country? Draw a picture below of a unique food, clothing or music that represents this country.

What is the climate like in this country? What are the most notable features of physical geography, such as mountain ranges, bodies of water, etc?

Now that you've learned more about this country, write a prayer below for the people who live there:

_____
_____
_____
_____
_____
_____
_____
_____
_____
_____
_____
_____
_____
_____
_____
_____
_____
_____
_____

MEET A MISSIONARY

Contact a missionary who is currently serving in one of the countries you just studied. Write down three questions you will ask and their answers below.

Missionary's Name: _____
Country where they live: _____

Question 1: _____
_____?

Answer: _____
_____
_____
_____

Question 2: _____
_____?

Answer: _____
_____
_____
_____

Question 3: _____
_____?

Answer: _____
_____
_____
_____

Make sure to pray for the missionary and the needs they mentioned when the conversation is over!

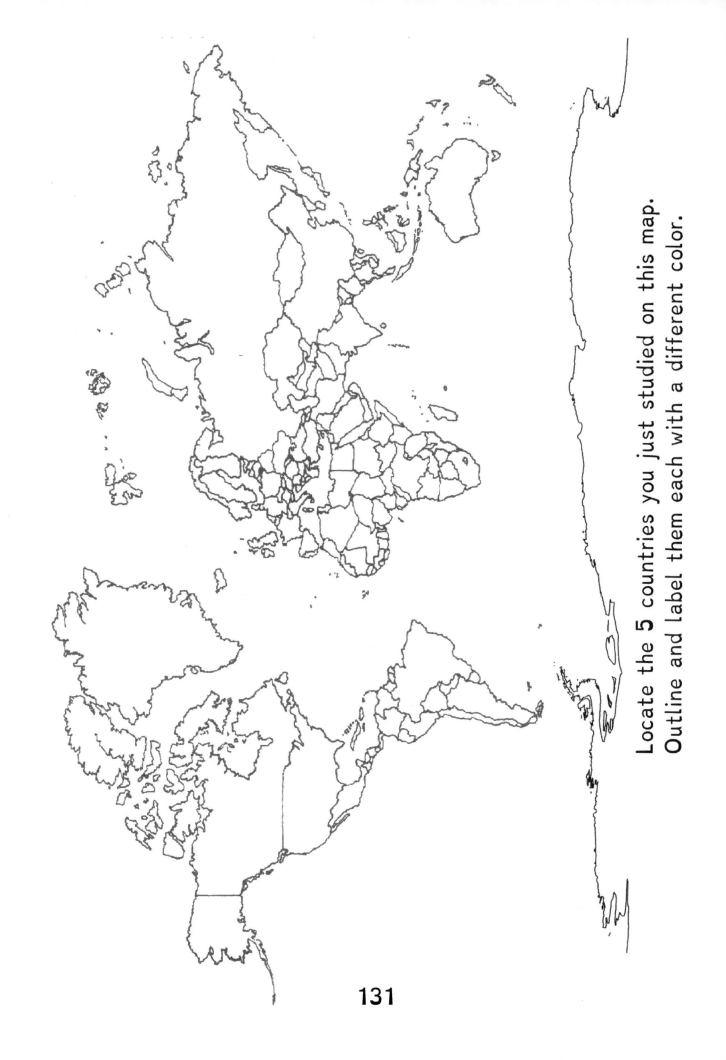

KAZAKHSTAN

Color the Flag

Language(s): _____
Continent: _____
Population: _____

Watch a video or read a book to learn more about this country, and write down one unique thing you learned:

_____
_____
_____
_____
_____
_____
_____
_____
_____

What are the major religions present in this country?
What percentage of the population does each represent?

_____   _____%
_____   _____%
_____   _____%
_____   _____%

What are the main challenges of living in this country?
What prayer needs do the people have?

_____
_____
_____
_____
_____
_____
_____
_____

What about this country can you praise God for?

_____
_____
_____
_____
_____
_____
_____

Use Google Earth to explore this country! Find the capital city and take a "walk" around. Draw a picture of something interesting you find below.

Capital: _____

Culture & Climate

What did you learn about the culture of this country? Draw a picture below of a unique food, clothing or music that represents this country.

What is the climate like in this country? What are the most notable features of physical geography, such as mountain ranges, bodies of water, etc?

Now that you've learned more about this country, write a prayer below for the people who live there:

_____
_____
_____
_____
_____
_____
_____
_____
_____
_____
_____
_____
_____
_____
_____
_____
_____

KENYA

Color the Flag

Language(s): _____
Continent: _____
Population: _____

Watch a video or read a book to learn more about this country, and write down one unique thing you learned:

_____
_____
_____
_____
_____
_____
_____
_____
_____

What are the major religions present in this country?
What percentage of the population does each represent?

_____	_____%
_____	_____%
_____	_____%
_____	_____%

What are the main challenges of living in this country? What prayer needs do the people have?

_____
_____
_____
_____
_____
_____
_____
_____
_____

What about this country can you praise God for?

_____
_____
_____
_____
_____
_____
_____
_____

Use Google Earth to explore this country! Find the capital city and take a "walk" around. Draw a picture of something interesting you find below.

Capital: _____

Culture & Climate

What did you learn about the culture of this country? Draw a picture below of a unique food, clothing or music that represents this country.

What is the climate like in this country? What are the most notable features of physical geography, such as mountain ranges, bodies of water, etc?

Now that you've learned more about this country, write a prayer below for the people who live there:

_____
_____
_____
_____
_____
_____
_____
_____
_____
_____
_____
_____
_____
_____
_____
_____

MEXICO

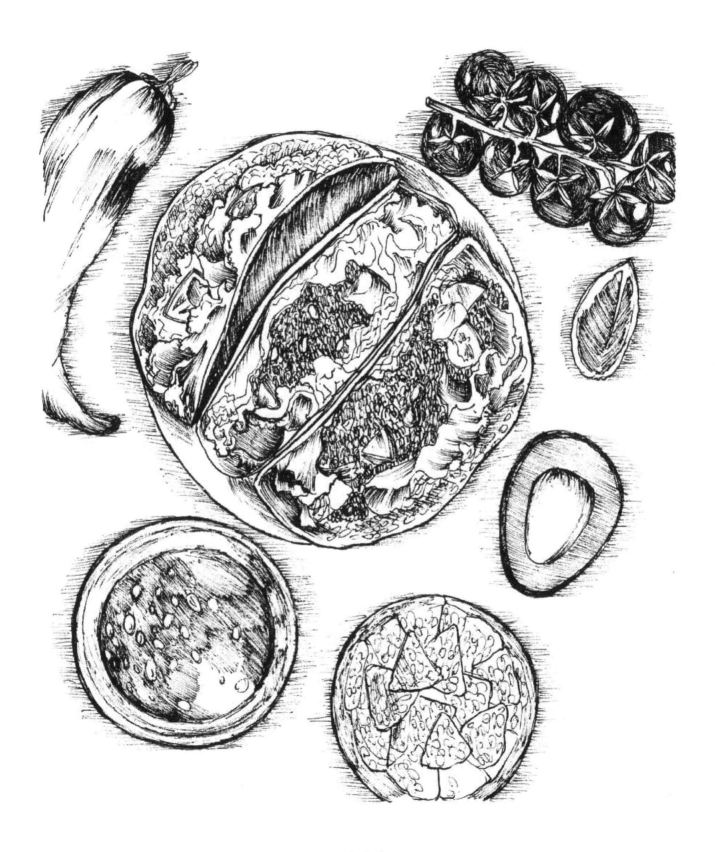

Color the Flag

Language(s): _____
Continent: _____
Population: _____

Watch a video or read a book to learn more about this country, and write down one unique thing you learned:

_____
_____
_____
_____
_____
_____
_____
_____
_____

What are the major religions present in this country?
What percentage of the population does each represent?

_____ _____%
_____ _____%
_____ _____%
_____ _____%

What are the main challenges of living in this country?
What prayer needs do the people have?

_____
_____
_____
_____
_____
_____
_____
_____

What about this country can you praise God for?

_____
_____
_____
_____
_____
_____
_____

Use Google Earth to explore this country! Find the capital city and take a "walk" around. Draw a picture of something interesting you find below.

Capital: _____

Culture & Climate

What did you learn about the culture of this country? Draw a picture below of a unique food, clothing or music that represents this country.

What is the climate like in this country? What are the most notable features of physical geography, such as mountain ranges, bodies of water, etc?

Now that you've learned more about this country, write a prayer below for the people who live there:

NORTH KOREA

Color the Flag

Language(s): _____
Continent: _____
Population: _____

Watch a video or read a book to learn more about this country, and write down one unique thing you learned:

_____
_____
_____
_____
_____
_____
_____
_____
_____
_____

What are the major religions present in this country?
What percentage of the population does each represent?

_____   _____%
_____   _____%
_____   _____%
_____   _____%

What are the main challenges of living in this country?
What prayer needs do the people have?

_____
_____
_____
_____
_____
_____
_____
_____

What about this country can you praise God for?

_____
_____
_____
_____
_____
_____
_____

Use Google Earth to explore this country! Find the capital city and take a "walk" around. Draw a picture of something interesting you find below.

Capital: _____

Culture & Climate

What did you learn about the culture of this country? Draw a picture below of a unique food, clothing or music that represents this country.

What is the climate like in this country? What are the most notable features of physical geography, such as mountain ranges, bodies of water, etc?

Now that you've learned more about this country, write a prayer below for the people who live there:

PAKISTAN

Color the Flag

Language(s): _____
Continent: _____
Population: _____

Watch a video or read a book to learn more about this country, and write down one unique thing you learned:

What are the major religions present in this country?
What percentage of the population does each represent?

_____	_____%
_____	_____%
_____	_____%
_____	_____%

What are the main challenges of living in this country?
What prayer needs do the people have?

_____
_____
_____
_____
_____
_____
_____
_____

What about this country can you praise God for?

_____
_____
_____
_____
_____
_____
_____
_____

Use Google Earth to explore this country! Find the capital city and take a "walk" around. Draw a picture of something interesting you find below.

Capital: _____

Culture & Climate

What did you learn about the culture of this country? Draw a picture below of a unique food, clothing or music that represents this country.

What is the climate like in this country? What are the most notable features of physical geography, such as mountain ranges, bodies of water, etc?

Now that you've learned more about this country, write a prayer below for the people who live there:

MEET A MISSIONARY

Contact a missionary who is currently serving in one of the countries you just studied. Write down three questions you will ask and their answers below.

Missionary's Name: _____

Country where they live: _____

Question 1: _____
_____?

Answer: _____
_____
_____
_____

Question 2: _____
_____?

Answer: _____
_____
_____
_____

Question 3: _____
_____?

Answer: _____
_____
_____
_____

Make sure to pray for the missionary and the needs they mentioned when the conversation is over!

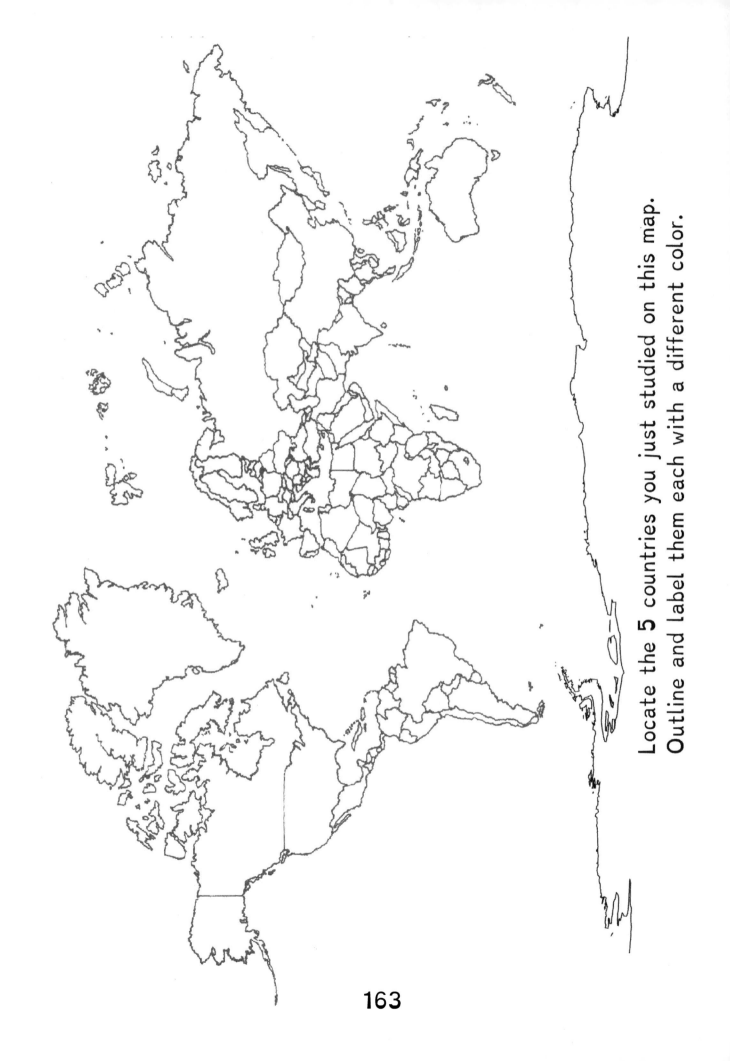

PERU

Color the Flag

Language(s): _____
Continent: _____
Population: _____

Watch a video or read a book to learn more about this country, and write down one unique thing you learned:

_____
_____
_____
_____
_____
_____
_____
_____
_____

What are the major religions present in this country?
What percentage of the population does each represent?

_____   _____%
_____   _____%
_____   _____%
_____   _____%

What are the main challenges of living in this country?
What prayer needs do the people have?

_____
_____
_____
_____
_____
_____
_____
_____
_____

What about this country can you praise God for?

_____
_____
_____
_____
_____
_____
_____

Use Google Earth to explore this country! Find the capital city and take a "walk" around. Draw a picture of something interesting you find below.

Capital: _____

Culture & Climate

What did you learn about the culture of this country? Draw a picture below of a unique food, clothing or music that represents this country.

What is the climate like in this country? What are the most notable features of physical geography, such as mountain ranges, bodies of water, etc?

Now that you've learned more about this country, write a prayer below for the people who live there:

_____
_____
_____
_____
_____
_____
_____
_____
_____
_____
_____
_____
_____
_____
_____
_____
_____

PHILIPPINES

Color the Flag

Language(s): _____
Continent: _____
Population: _____

Watch a video or read a book to learn more about this country, and write down one unique thing you learned:

_____
_____
_____
_____
_____
_____
_____
_____
_____

What are the major religions present in this country?
What percentage of the population does each represent?

_____   _____%
_____   _____%
_____   _____%
_____   _____%

What are the main challenges of living in this country?
What prayer needs do the people have?

_____
_____
_____
_____
_____
_____
_____
_____
_____

What about this country can you praise God for?

_____
_____
_____
_____
_____
_____
_____
_____

Use Google Earth to explore this country! Find the capital city and take a "walk" around. Draw a picture of something interesting you find below.

Capital: _____

Culture & Climate

What did you learn about the culture of this country? Draw a picture below of a unique food, clothing or music that represents this country.

What is the climate like in this country? What are the most notable features of physical geography, such as mountain ranges, bodies of water, etc?

Now that you've learned more about this country, write a prayer below for the people who live there:

UKRAINE

Color the Flag

Language(s): _____
Continent: _____
Population: _____

Watch a video or read a book to learn more about this country, and write down one unique thing you learned:

_____
_____
_____
_____
_____
_____
_____
_____
_____
_____

What are the major religions present in this country?
What percentage of the population does each represent?

_____	_____%
_____	_____%
_____	_____%
_____	_____%

What are the main challenges of living in this country?
What prayer needs do the people have?

_____
_____
_____
_____
_____
_____
_____
_____

What about this country can you praise God for?

_____
_____
_____
_____
_____
_____
_____
_____

Use Google Earth to explore this country! Find the capital city and take a "walk" around. Draw a picture of something interesting you find below.

Capital: _____

Culture & Climate

What did you learn about the culture of this country? Draw a picture below of a unique food, clothing or music that represents this country.

What is the climate like in this country? What are the most notable features of physical geography, such as mountain ranges, bodies of water, etc?

Now that you've learned more about this country, write a prayer below for the people who live there:

YEMEN

Color the Flag

Language(s): _____
Continent: _____
Population: _____

Watch a video or read a book to learn more about this country, and write down one unique thing you learned:

_____
_____
_____
_____
_____
_____
_____
_____
_____

What are the major religions present in this country?
What percentage of the population does each represent?

_____	_____%
_____	_____%
_____	_____%
_____	_____%

What are the main challenges of living in this country? What prayer needs do the people have?

_____
_____
_____
_____
_____
_____
_____
_____
_____

What about this country can you praise God for?

_____
_____
_____
_____
_____
_____
_____
_____

Use Google Earth to explore this country! Find the capital city and take a "walk" around. Draw a picture of something interesting you find below.

Capital: _____

Culture & Climate

What did you learn about the culture of this country? Draw a picture below of a unique food, clothing or music that represents this country.

What is the climate like in this country? What are the most notable features of physical geography, such as mountain ranges, bodies of water, etc?

Now that you've learned more about this country, write a prayer below for the people who live there:

ZAMBIA

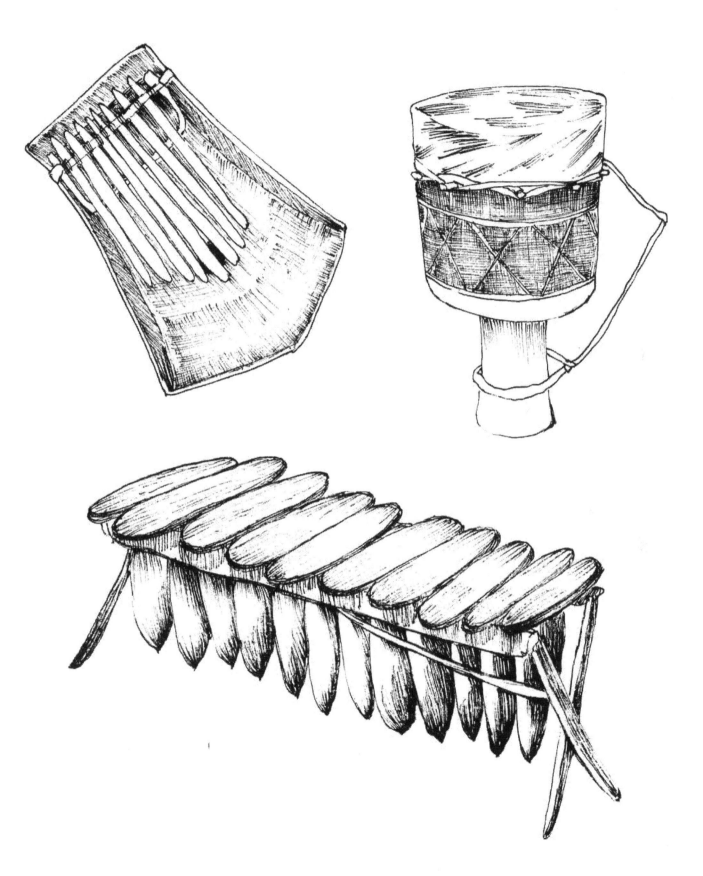

Color the Flag

Language(s): _____
Continent: _____
Population: _____

Watch a video or read a book to learn more about this country, and write down one unique thing you learned:

_____
_____
_____
_____
_____
_____
_____
_____
_____
_____

What are the major religions present in this country?
What percentage of the population does each represent?

_____   _____%
_____   _____%
_____   _____%
_____   _____%

What are the main challenges of living in this country?
What prayer needs do the people have?

_____
_____
_____
_____
_____
_____
_____
_____
_____

What about this country can you praise God for?

_____
_____
_____
_____
_____
_____
_____
_____

Use Google Earth to explore this country! Find the capital city and take a "walk" around. Draw a picture of something interesting you find below.

Capital: _____

Culture & Climate

What did you learn about the culture of this country? Draw a picture below of a unique food, clothing or music that represents this country.

What is the climate like in this country? What are the most notable features of physical geography, such as mountain ranges, bodies of water, etc?

Now that you've learned more about this country, write a prayer below for the people who live there:

_____
_____
_____
_____
_____
_____
_____
_____
_____
_____
_____
_____
_____
_____
_____
_____
_____
_____
_____
_____

MEET A MISSIONARY

Contact a missionary who is currently serving in one of the countries you just studied. Write down three questions you will ask and their answers below.

Missionary's Name: _____
Country where they live: _____

Question 1: _____
_____?

Answer: _____
_____
_____
_____

Question 2: _____
_____?

Answer: _____
_____
_____
_____

Question 3: _____
_____?

Answer: _____
_____
_____
_____

Make sure to pray for the missionary and the needs they mentioned when the conversation is over!

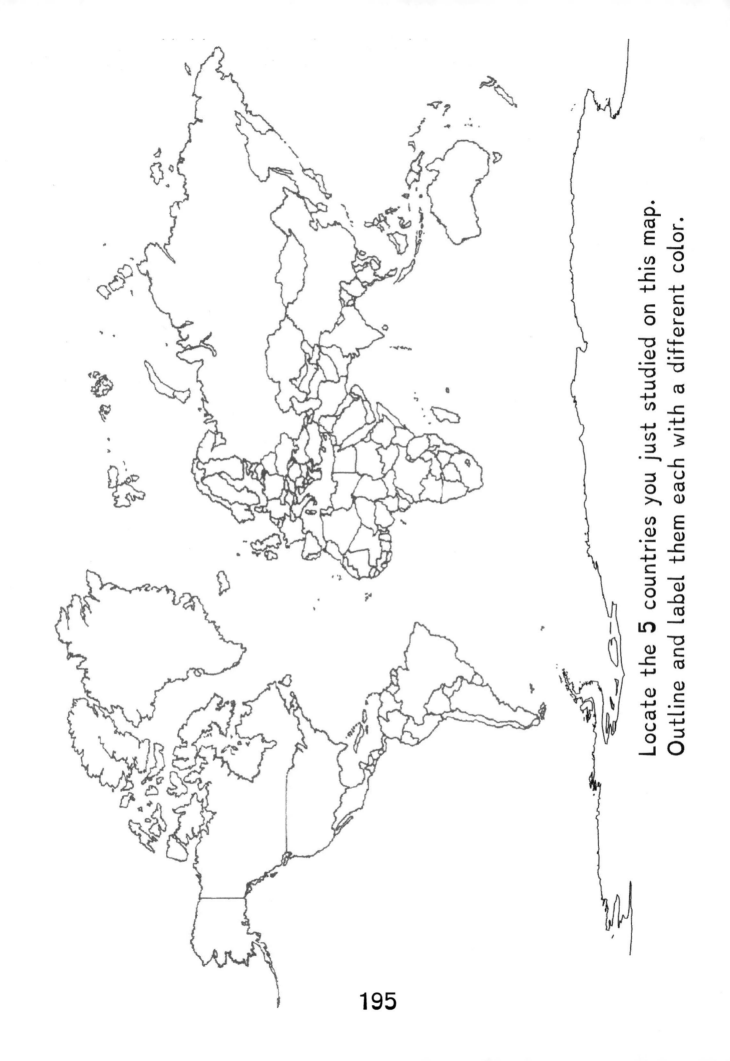

Locate the 5 countries you just studied on this map. Outline and label them each with a different color.

195

CHOOSE YOUR OWN COUNTRY

——————————————————

Draw a picture below to represent this country:

Color the Flag

Language(s): _____
Continent: _____
Population: _____

Watch a video or read a book to learn more about this country, and write down one unique thing you learned:

What are the major religions present in this country?
What percentage of the population does each represent?

Religion	%
_____	_____%
_____	_____%
_____	_____%
_____	_____%

What are the main challenges of living in this country?
What prayer needs do the people have?

_____
_____
_____
_____
_____
_____
_____
_____
_____

What about this country can you praise God for?

_____
_____
_____
_____
_____
_____
_____
_____

Use Google Earth to explore this country! Find the capital city and take a "walk" around. Draw a picture of something interesting you find below.

Capital: _____

Culture & Climate

What did you learn about the culture of this country? Draw a picture below of a unique food, clothing or music that represents this country.

What is the climate like in this country? What are the most notable features of physical geography, such as mountain ranges, bodies of water, etc?

Now that you've learned more about this country, write a prayer below for the people who live there:

_____
_____
_____
_____
_____
_____
_____
_____
_____
_____
_____
_____
_____
_____
_____
_____
_____
_____
_____
_____

CHOOSE YOUR OWN COUNTRY

Draw a picture below to represent this country:

Color the Flag

Language(s): _____
Continent: _____
Population: _____

Watch a video or read a book to learn more about this country, and write down one unique thing you learned:

What are the major religions present in this country?
What percentage of the population does each represent?

_____   _____%
_____   _____%
_____   _____%
_____   _____%

What are the main challenges of living in this country?
What prayer needs do the people have?

_____
_____
_____
_____
_____
_____
_____
_____

What about this country can you praise God for?

_____
_____
_____
_____
_____
_____
_____

Use Google Earth to explore this country! Find the capital city and take a "walk" around. Draw a picture of something interesting you find below.

Capital: _____

Culture & Climate

What did you learn about the culture of this country? Draw a picture below of a unique food, clothing or music that represents this country.

What is the climate like in this country? What are the most notable features of physical geography, such as mountain ranges, bodies of water, etc?

Now that you've learned more about this country, write a prayer below for the people who live there:

_____
_____
_____
_____
_____
_____
_____
_____
_____
_____
_____
_____
_____
_____
_____
_____
_____
_____
_____

CHOOSE YOUR OWN COUNTRY

_____

Draw a picture below to represent this country:

Color the Flag

Language(s): _____
Continent: _____
Population: _____

Watch a video or read a book to learn more about this country, and write down one unique thing you learned:

_____
_____
_____
_____
_____
_____
_____
_____
_____

What are the major religions present in this country?
What percentage of the population does each represent?

_____	_____%
_____	_____%
_____	_____%
_____	_____%

What are the main challenges of living in this country?
What prayer needs do the people have?

_____
_____
_____
_____
_____
_____
_____
_____

What about this country can you praise God for?

_____
_____
_____
_____
_____
_____
_____
_____

Use Google Earth to explore this country! Find the capital city and take a "walk" around. Draw a picture of something interesting you find below.

Capital: _____

Culture & Climate

What did you learn about the culture of this country? Draw a picture below of a unique food, clothing or music that represents this country.

What is the climate like in this country? What are the most notable features of physical geography, such as mountain ranges, bodies of water, etc?

Now that you've learned more about this country, write a prayer below for the people who live there:

_____
_____
_____
_____
_____
_____
_____
_____
_____
_____
_____
_____
_____
_____
_____
_____
_____
_____
_____
_____

CHOOSE YOUR OWN COUNTRY

Draw a picture below to represent this country:

Color the Flag

Language(s): _____
Continent: _____
Population: _____

Watch a video or read a book to learn more about this country, and write down one unique thing you learned:

_____
_____
_____
_____
_____
_____
_____
_____
_____

What are the major religions present in this country?
What percentage of the population does each represent?

_____   _____%
_____   _____%
_____   _____%
_____   _____%

What are the main challenges of living in this country? What prayer needs do the people have?

_____
_____
_____
_____
_____
_____
_____
_____
_____

What about this country can you praise God for?

_____
_____
_____
_____
_____
_____
_____
_____

Use Google Earth to explore this country! Find the capital city and take a "walk" around. Draw a picture of something interesting you find below.

Capital: _____

Culture & Climate

What did you learn about the culture of this country? Draw a picture below of a unique food, clothing or music that represents this country.

What is the climate like in this country? What are the most notable features of physical geography, such as mountain ranges, bodies of water, etc?

Now that you've learned more about this country, write a prayer below for the people who live there:

_____
_____
_____
_____
_____
_____
_____
_____
_____
_____
_____
_____
_____
_____
_____
_____
_____
_____
_____

CHOOSE YOUR OWN COUNTRY

_____

Draw a picture below to represent this country:

Color the Flag

Language(s): _____
Continent: _____
Population: _____

Watch a video or read a book to learn more about this country, and write down one unique thing you learned:

_____
_____
_____
_____
_____
_____
_____
_____
_____

What are the major religions present in this country?
What percentage of the population does each represent?

_____	_____%
_____	_____%
_____	_____%
_____	_____%

What are the main challenges of living in this country?
What prayer needs do the people have?

_____
_____
_____
_____
_____
_____
_____
_____
_____

What about this country can you praise God for?

_____
_____
_____
_____
_____
_____
_____
_____

Use Google Earth to explore this country! Find the capital city and take a "walk" around. Draw a picture of something interesting you find below.

Capital: _____

Culture & Climate

What did you learn about the culture of this country? Draw a picture below of a unique food, clothing or music that represents this country.

What is the climate like in this country? What are the most notable features of physical geography, such as mountain ranges, bodies of water, etc?

Now that you've learned more about this country, write a prayer below for the people who live there:

_____
_____
_____
_____
_____
_____
_____
_____
_____
_____
_____
_____
_____
_____
_____
_____
_____
_____
_____

MEET A MISSIONARY

Contact a missionary who is currently serving in one of the countries you just studied. Write down three questions you will ask and their answers below.

Missionary's Name: _____
Country where they live: _____

Question 1: _____
_____?

Answer: _____
_____
_____
_____

Question 2: _____
_____?

Answer: _____
_____
_____
_____

Question 3: _____
_____?

Answer: _____
_____
_____
_____

Make sure to pray for the missionary and the needs they mentioned when the conversation is over!

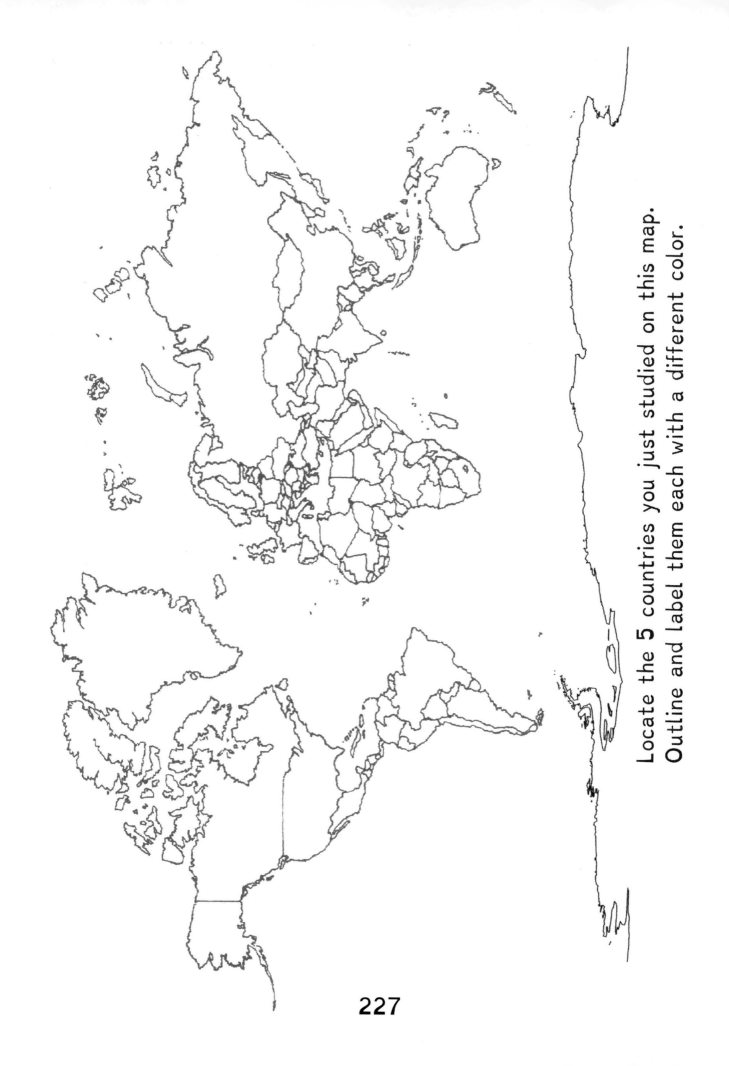

Locate the 5 countries you just studied on this map. Outline and label them each with a different color.

MISSIONARY BIOGRAPHY

Read or watch a biography of a missionary and write what you learn below.

Missionary's Name: _____
Country where they served: _____

What were the challenges this missionary faced?
_____
_____
_____
_____
_____
_____

How did God work through this missionary?
_____
_____
_____
_____
_____

What character traits do you see in this missionary that you should emulate in your own life?
_____
_____
_____
_____
_____

MISSIONARY BIOGRAPHY

Read or watch a biography of a missionary and write what you learn below.

Missionary's Name: _____
Country where they served: _____

What were the challenges this missionary faced?

_____
_____
_____
_____
_____
_____

How did God work through this missionary?

_____
_____
_____
_____
_____
_____

What character traits do you see in this missionary that you should emulate in your own life?

_____
_____
_____
_____
_____

MISSIONARY BIOGRAPHY

Read or watch a biography of a missionary and write what you learn below.

Missionary's Name: _____
Country where they served: _____

What were the challenges this missionary faced?
_____
_____
_____
_____
_____
_____

How did God work through this missionary?
_____
_____
_____
_____
_____
_____

What character traits do you see in this missionary that you should emulate in your own life?
_____
_____
_____
_____
_____

Made in United States
Orlando, FL
25 April 2022